A STEP-BY STEP G

# LIVING
## INTENTIONALLY

**How to be Intentional in Your Life through
Awareness, Clarity, Action, and Growth**

Dedicated to my friends and family who continuously support me
in my passion to help others achieve their greatness

*"Whoever believes in me, as the Scripture has said,
streams of living water will flow from within him."*
*— John 7:38*

# AMY WATTS

Your Encouragement Coach

A Step-by-Step Guide to

# LIVING INTENTIONALLY

How to be Intentional in Your Life through
Awareness, Clarity, Action, and Growth

*A special thanks to my editor and cover designer, Laura New. We were perfectly matched to bring this book to life.*

Vision Plan Grow Publishers

E-Mail amy@visionplangrow.com

Visit www.visonplangrow.com to learn more!

ISBN: 978-0692124987

I Believe in You!

# CONTENTS

# WELCOME TO YOUR GROWTH PLANNER

*...where everything BIG starts with something small.*

Congratulations! In beginning this workbook, you have made the first small step towards your "Growth to Living Intentionally." I am so excited for you. You are ready and now have included tools that will help you achieve your desired outcomes. You have what it takes. It is your time, and the time is now!

## So, let's get started to "Vision Plan Grow to Living Intentionally."

Remember living intentionally is a journey, NOT a destination. Yes, you can celebrate end points as you achieve them; however, the process of envisioning, planning, and growing never ends on this earth. Do not become attached to your desires; instead, know you are growing in life by being intentional in what fulfills you and brings you joy. This is a life you deserve and a life worth living!

## If you are not growing, you are dying.

In this beautiful and ever-changing world, it is easy to get side-tracked. You sometimes seek fulfillment in material goods or achievements. You might get caught up in others' actions or thoughts. You compare yourself. Many times, you feel so overwhelmed that you settle for less than what you really want or really deserve. You stay in your comfort zone and then wonder why nothing changes. You may just purely exist.

## You were not created to just exist. You were given gifts. Be intentional about them.

Know that slowing down is healthy and sometimes actually <u>more</u> productive. Life is not a race. Be intentional about each day by moving forward, taking action, and then just being. Know you are planting the seeds to bear fruit. Have faith and trust that success will come to you.

You will use the following 4 Key Tools to help provide you the awareness, clarity, focus, and step-by-step process to being intentional in core areas of your life:

1. **Life Assessment Tool** – To reflect on where you are today through a scoring system.

2. **Growth Ring Tool** – To identify areas that you want to improve or work on to grow. You then set 1-3 goals for growth in those areas and explanations about why you chose them.

3. **Growth Tree Tool (Vision Board)** – To create a tangible image of where you want to be through a visualization and writing tool.

4. **My Legacy Letter** – To write a letter to your loved ones about your values, beliefs, and memories for them to remember you by.

## I truly BELIEVE in YOU!

With Love,

*Amy*

# STORY

You started as a small seed planted in your mother's womb. Each year you celebrate is another year of growth that becomes your story in this book of life. Many see your external growth like that of a tree; however, your internal growth is what truly tells the story and defines you.

A growing tree also once started as a tiny seed, planted and nurtured. A tree has growth rings that share the story of its life. Externally you see the trees' growth with luscious branches full of leaves, but the growth rings inside truly tell its story.

This Growth Planner is your step-by-step guide to being intentional about not only your external growth but also your internal growth. It provides you tools with practical, highly effective, and proven methods coaches use.

The key to success is to be patient and focus on what you can control. No one plants a seed and then expects a tree the next day. Rather, for that tree to grow, the seed must receive water, sunlight, and nutrients from a healthy environment. The same goes for you if you want to grow. Here are 5 habits that are necessary for you to grow intentionally:

1. **Positive Attitude** – The sun never stops shining even during the storms. It may be hidden, but it still rises. Sunlight is essential for growth. Your daily attitude is like the sun. When you rise each day, ensure you have a positive attitude. Even when you experience challenges, find the "silver linings" in the storms.

2. **Daily Agenda** – Your daily agenda is like watering the soil. You can't see the seed growing under the soil, but taking small actions daily helps grow your plan and desires. In this daily agenda, be flexible and flowing. If some things don't occur on your time, don't get disappointed, just keep moving forward. Find happiness in the process and growth. It will come in its right time.

3. **Healthy Environment** – A seed won't grow in a basement with no soil and light. Neither will you. Plant yourself in a healthy environment. Surround yourself by others who will help you grow, support you, inspire you, and love you. Also, take time and care for yourself!

4. **Reflect** – Reflect on your progress for accountability and maintaining awareness. When you reflect, you may identify better resources to help you grow or realize that you may need to change some things to keep growing.

5. **Express Gratitude** – Take time to recognize your growth and achievements. Celebrate them with gratitude. Know everything BIG starts with something small.

*As you grow...don't forget to share with others. Many just see the external growth, but the moments that truly define and grow you are the ones on the inside that tell the story!*

# 1 LIFE ASSESSMENT TOOL

**WITH THIS TOOL YOU WILL:**

- Establish a baseline of where you are today

- Use a guided assessment to score core areas of life

- Reflect on your scores and create awareness with questions

- Repeat every six months to measure changes and growth

---

*"It doesn't matter where you are coming from. All that matters is where you are going."* — BRIAN TRACY

---

Every form of growth should start with a self-assessment to help you establish where you are today. This exercise provides a baseline to measure your growth in areas of your life where you recognize changes are needed to reach your desired outcome.

After completing this assessment, you should have more clarity and awareness on the areas you want to move or change. You are provided additional questions to help narrow your focus, identify real issues, and recognize roadblocks getting in the way.

In this area, we are sometimes not honest with ourselves, which can hold us back from achieving our desired outcomes. Make sure you take your time and be truthful with yourself. No one ever succeeded by deceiving himself.

# LIFE ASSESSMENT

There are no wrong answers and no grade, only your own thoughtful assessment. Be honest and truthful to yourself. Even if the truth is painful or embarrassing, remember that no one else needs to see it and you will never succeed by deceiving yourself.

Score yourself from 1 to 10 (10 being highest/fully fulfilled in area). Start with the NOW column. You will check in and re-evaluate at six months and again at one year.

|  | NOW | 6 MONTHS | 1 YEAR |
|---|---|---|---|
| How satisfied are you with your LIFE OVERALL? | /10 | /10 | /10 |
|  |  |  |  |
| How happy are you in your current CAREER? | /10 | /10 | /10 |
|  |  |  |  |
| How well do your current FINANCES fulfill your needs? | /10 | /10 | /10 |
|  |  |  |  |
| How satisfied are you with your HOME ENVIRONMENT? | /10 | /10 | /10 |
|  |  |  |  |
| How do you feel about your SELF-IMAGE and LOVING YOURSELF? | /10 | /10 | /10 |
|  |  |  |  |
| How satisfied are you with your quality time with FAMILY & FRIENDS? | /10 | /10 | /10 |
|  |  |  |  |
| How do you feel about your HEALTH & WELLNESS? | /10 | /10 | /10 |
|  |  |  |  |
| How happy are you with your personal GROWTH and DEVELOPMENT? | /10 | /10 | /10 |
|  |  |  |  |
| How satisfied are you with your SPIRITUALITY or CONNECTION to SPIRITUAL SOURCE? | /10 | /10 | /10 |
|  |  |  |  |
| How do you feel about your MARRIAGE or RELATIONSHIP? | /10 | /10 | /10 |
|  |  |  |  |
| How happy are you with your ability to CONTRIBUTE to others or society? | /10 | /10 | /10 |
|  |  |  |  |
| How satisfied are you with your FUN & RECREATION? | /10 | /10 | /10 |
|  |  |  |  |

# HERE ARE QUESTIONS TO ASK YOURSELF:

1.  How do you feel about your life as you look at your assessment?

    _____

    _____

    _____

2.  Is there anything that surprises you?

    _____

    _____

    _____

3.  Which of these areas would you most like to improve? (Choose 1-3.)

    _____

    _____

    _____

4.  What help, support, or resources might you need to make changes?

    _____

    _____

    _____

5.  Which areas are you most satisfied with?

    _____

    _____

    _____

6.  What change should you make first? **Why** do you want to make this change?

    _____

    _____

    _____

7.  What won't you let get in your way of taking action? Are you **ALL** in?

    _____

    _____

    _____

# NOTES:

# ② GROWTH RING TOOL

## WITH THIS TOOL YOU WILL:

- Map out your life assessment scores on the Growth Ring Tool

- Provide a visual snapshot of how satisfied you are in core areas of life and visually recognize areas that may need attention or growth

- Set goals in areas you want to be intentional about growing

- Establish your Top 3 Yearly Goals and define your "why"

- Break down your Top 3 Yearly Goals into daily/weekly actions

*"If you focus on results, you will never change. If you focus on change you will get results."* — JACK DIXON

The Growth Ring raises awareness and allows you to reflect visually on how satisfied and intentional you are in core areas of your life. Your completed Growth Ring may not be fully round but rather uneven and non-uniform. This shape allows you to identify areas where you are excelling or that may need more attention. Ultimately, your goal should be to grow areas that need more commitment to create satisfaction in your life.

Ensure you work to *grow* your ring, not trade off some areas of your life to improve others. This is about moving forward, challenging yourself, and pushing your boundaries to *expand* your growth ring and make it *bigger* while maintaining a *balance*.

Commit to yourself and <u>take action</u> TODAY!

What specific actions or steps will you take to enhance your satisfaction in your desired area? Write 1-3 actions you will take in the boxes on the growth ring above each area.

Then choose your Top 3 Areas you want to grow and explain "why" you desire to grow these areas. Break them down into small actions (baby steps) over the year that will help you accomplish them. It's ok if you don't know all of the actions now. Start with one if that helps, and then as you complete it, you can add another.

Keep your Growth Ring close to you in a place that you can easily refer to and reflect on a daily basis.

Track your progress! This visual tool provides a snapshot in time of your growth. It ensures you are paying attention to the most important areas of your life and will help you stay focused on taking action towards living a satisfied life. I recommend reviewing and updating your Growth Ring at least once every six months, depending on your goals and your target timeline for achieving them.

Over the years you will be able to see visually how your personal Growth Ring has been challenged and how it grows like that of a tree's growth rings.

---

## EXAMPLE OF WHAT A GROWTH RING MAY LOOK LIKE

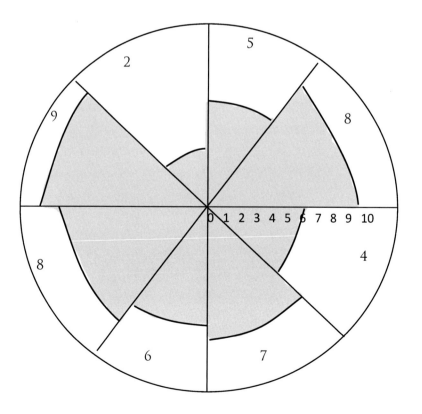

# YEARLY GROWTH RING EXERCISE

The purpose of this tool is to raise your awareness and allow you to reflect on core areas of your life where you would like to be more intentional. For each area, enter 1-3 goals in the box that you would like to grow this year. These are your BIG goals. The vision of writing these down is the first small step to moving towards them.

Then, using your Life Assessment from Chapter 1 for reference, highlight in the growth area where you rate yourself from 1 -10. The center represents "0" and the outer, bold line represents "10."

Next, choose the **Top 3** that will be your focus to grow this year. Then, share your "**why**" for that growth area.

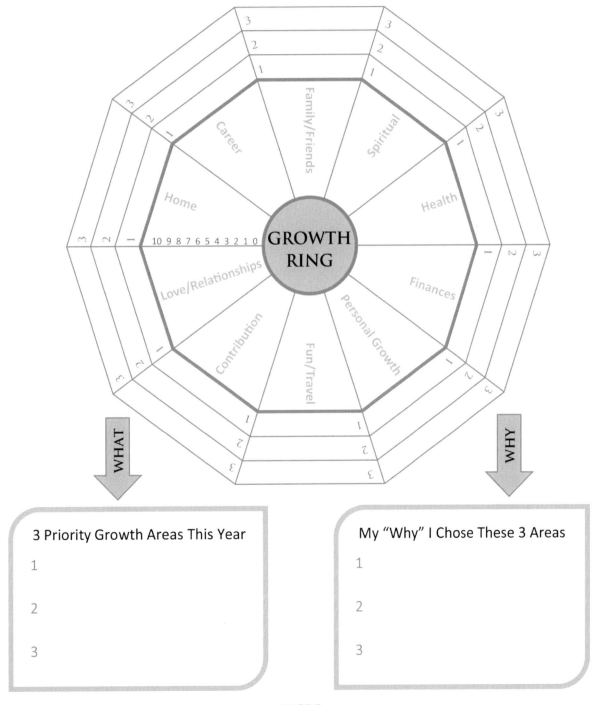

# NOTES:

# 3 Top Goals & Action Plan

Now, map out the actions needed to move towards and achieve your Top 3 Growth Areas this year. Start with small, realistic, daily, or weekly actions. Getting started is the hardest part, which is why small and attainable actions are key to move you. Then once **you get started, you will build momentum.** Note that many people find it easier to focus on a few goals only at first, and then add more if needed as the year progresses.

## GOAL #1: _____

Accomplish By: _____ Goal Complete: ☐

### Actions to Accomplish My Goal:

1. _____ 4. _____

2. _____ 5. _____

3. _____ 6. _____

## GOAL #2: _____

Accomplish By: _____ Goal Complete: ☐

### Actions to Accomplish My Goal:

1. _____ 4. _____

2. _____ 5. _____

3. _____ 6. _____

## GOAL #3: _____

Accomplish By: _____ Goal Complete: ☐

### Actions to Accomplish My Goal:

1. _____ 4. _____

2. _____ 5. _____

3. _____ 6. _____

# Top Goals & Action Plan

Additional Goal Sheets

## Goal #4: _____

Accomplish By: _____ Goal Complete: ☐

### Actions to Accomplish My Goal:

1. _____    4. _____

2. _____    5. _____

3. _____    6. _____

## Goal #5: _____

Accomplish By: _____ Goal Complete: ☐

### Actions to Accomplish My Goal:

1. _____    4. _____

2. _____    5. _____

3. _____    6. _____

## Goal #6: _____

Accomplish By: _____ Goal Complete: ☐

### Actions to Accomplish My Goal:

1. _____    4. _____

2. _____    5. _____

3. _____    6. _____

# TOP GOALS & ACTION PLAN

Additional Goal Sheets

## GOAL #7: _____

Accomplish By: _____    Goal Complete: ☐

### Actions to Accomplish My Goal:

1. _____    4. _____

2. _____    5. _____

3. _____    6. _____


## GOAL #8: _____

Accomplish By: _____    Goal Complete: ☐

### Actions to Accomplish My Goal:

1. _____    4. _____

2. _____    5. _____

3. _____    6. _____


## GOAL #9: _____

Accomplish By: _____    Goal Complete: ☐

### Actions to Accomplish My Goal:

1. _____    4. _____

2. _____    5. _____

3. _____    6. _____

# 3 GROWTH TREE

■■ ■ ■■ ■ ■ ■ ■■ ■ ■ ■ ■■ ■ ■ ■ ■■ ■ ■ ■■

## WITH THIS TOOL YOU WILL:

- Create a Growth Tree with all your goals, dreams, and inspirations

- Affirm the type of environment in which to plant yourself to promote growth

- Establish what values you won't compromise in order to grow

- Write a letter to yourself as if you are one year in the future looking back at all you have achieved

- Use the Habit Tracker to attract your vision and renew your mind towards your goals and desires

■ ■ ■ ■ ■ ■ ■ ■ ■ ■ ■ ■ ■ ■ ■ ■ ■ ■ ■ ■ ■ ■

*"Vision without action is a daydream. Action without vision is a nightmare."* — JAPANESE PROVERB

Visualization and imagination are extremely important to achieving your goals and dreams. If you do not take time to visualize your end results, they can quickly become a distant memory. The Growth Tree Tool gives you an actual picture of your goals and what they look like for you. Seeing goals this way often leads to believing in them; believing in goals often leads to achieving them.

In this busy world, we sometimes lose ourselves and forget to dream, imagine, and envision our desires. We stick close to what we know and stay comfortable. Did you know that imagination has a physiological impact on your emotions? Your body reacts with physical symptoms to the images provided by your mind. Often, mental practice can get you closer to where you want to be in life and prepare you for success.

Just doing this exercise can enhance motivation, increase confidence, improve performance, and prime your brain for success.

The environment in which you plant yourself is another key factor to your success and growth. In this exercise, make sure you share what type of environment you need to be surrounded by to grow. It can include people, emotions, attitude, resources, home life, etc. Take time to know what that environment is and how to ensure you maintain it or find your way back to it when off track. Also, know what values or ethics you will not compromise as you grow into the best you. Although sacrifices and commitments may stretch you, they should never cost you regrets or loss of essentials.

After creating your Growth Tree, your final exercise is a written vision of future. This stream of consciousness exercise will awaken the creative right side of your brain. You will write a letter to yourself as if it is *one year* from now, looking back and detailing your achievements and accomplishments from the last year. Be as descriptive as possible, as if these triumphs already happened. Make sure you put the future date and address it to yourself like a real letter. During this exercise, limit interruptions as much as possible. You will need 20-25 minutes to yourself of silence to help you tap into your "inner-self," listen, and write.

The goal is not to think hard but to write what *flows* through your mind using your imagination and being free from the limiting reality we live in. This exercise creates what can be and has no limits. If something odd should come to mind, write it down. Use scents, colors, and textures as you are there in the moment when writing. Let it allow you to feel alive, optimistic, and enthusiastic as you connect to the deeper part of yourself!

Once you complete this section of exercises, review and reflect on your Growth Tree and Vision of Future letter as often as possible. I recommend daily for at least the first 28 days. Keep it in a place where it is very accessible (perhaps a nightstand, desk, or refrigerator). I also recommend sharing it with others, as that will enhance and empower the Law of Attraction.

# GROWTH TREE VISION BOARD

If you could be anything, do anything, have anything, what would it be? This is your Growth Tree—
your Vision Board—where you can create a visual of the goals, dreams, and desires you want to
achieve. This tree can display all the goals you set in core areas of your life this year. There are no
limits! You can place actual pictures, cut out words, draw, or write what you envision in each leaf. This
tree, like that of a real tree, represents all the growth you want to achieve in the next year. Have fun!

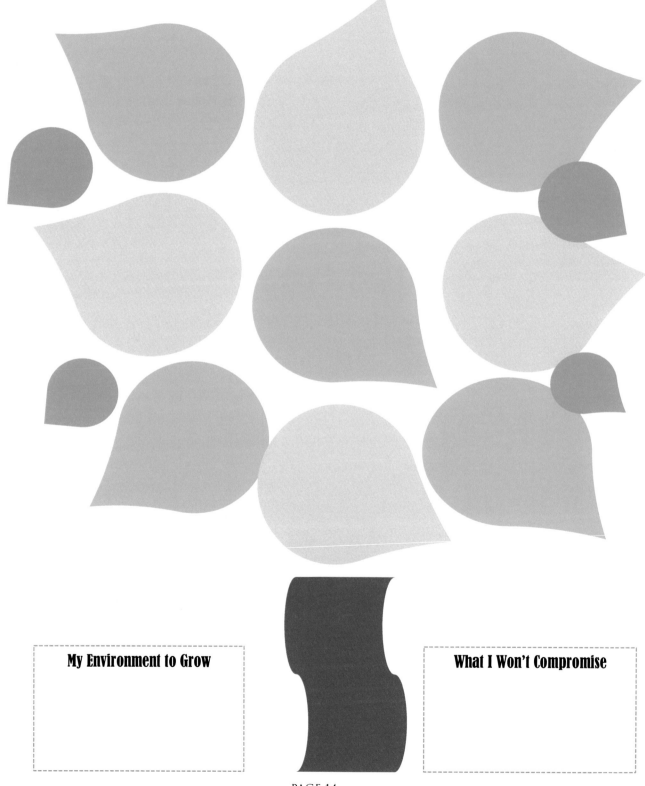

My Environment to Grow

What I Won't Compromise

# Vision of Future – Written Exercise

Visualize yourself one year from now and write a letter back to yourself as if you achieved all your desires. Include anything and everything that resonates. Write as if you already achieved your goals.

# VISION OF FUTURE – WRITTEN EXERCISE

# Vision of Future – Written Exercise

# Must Do:

This sheet is a place to track your daily reflection of your Growth Tree and Vision of Future letter. In the box and note page, add any detail or clarity you receive each time you re-read your vision.

I cannot stress enough the importance of READING, BELIEVING, and SEEING your vision as a reality daily for the first 28 days, and as often as you like after that time period.

You are a creative being. When you focus your mind on your goals and desires, your mind believes in them and you are pulled to create them into your reality. This is the most important action for those who want success and results, and it stems from the Universal Law of Vibration. According to it, you must vibrate on the same frequency of what you want to create. Through patience and persistence, you can grow into understanding and mastering this habit.

## Habit Tracker

Vision of Future Letter/Tree

| 1 | 2 | 3 | 4 | 5 | 6 | 7 |
|----|----|----|----|----|----|----|
| 8 | 9 | 10 | 11 | 12 | 13 | 14 |
| 15 | 16 | 17 | 18 | 19 | 20 | 21 |
| 22 | 23 | 24 | 25 | 26 | 27 | 28 |

| 1 | 2 | 3 | 4 | 5 | 6 | 7 |
|----|----|----|----|----|----|----|
| 8 | 9 | 10 | 11 | 12 | 13 | 14 |
| 15 | 16 | 17 | 18 | 19 | 20 | 21 |
| 22 | 23 | 24 | 25 | 26 | 27 | 28 |

| 1 | 2 | 3 | 4 | 5 | 6 | 7 |
|----|----|----|----|----|----|----|
| 8 | 9 | 10 | 11 | 12 | 13 | 14 |
| 15 | 16 | 17 | 18 | 19 | 20 | 21 |
| 22 | 23 | 24 | 25 | 26 | 27 | 28 |

## Any New Ideas or Additions to my Vision

# NOTES:

# 4 MY LEGACY LETTER

## WITH THIS TOOL YOU WILL:

- Grow in your awareness of how you want to be remembered

- Write a letter to communicate the legacy you want others to remember you by, sharing core values, stories, wisdom, favorite things, etc.

- Reflect on your letter as accountability to ensure you are living intentionally in your daily life to inspire and bless others

*"Our fingerprints don't fade from the lives we touch."*
— JUDY BLUME

We all hope to be remembered. A legacy letter is another tool to bring awareness and intentionality to how you are living your daily life.

Are you living your core values? Do you take time to share your wisdom, stories, and favorite things?

A legacy letter is used to discover, become aware, communicate, and live how you want to be remembered by those you love or your community. No matter your age or gender, legacy writing is a wonderful tool to help you grow in being intentional. It gives purpose to your daily life, nourishes you, and helps you appreciate yourself more deeply.

A legacy letter also preserves your family stories, history, and values that embody your most cherished principles. It is something worthwhile that may inspire and bless future generations. Even if you do not have family, it is a gift to yourself today and for those who will remember you tomorrow.

Here are 5 questions that may help you get started:

1.  What core values are you proud of and live by that are positive for you?

2.  Do you have a story, adversity, or memory that you want generations to remember?

3.  Are you proud of any big accomplishments in your life?

4.  Is there any advice, instructions, or quotes you want to make sure you share?

5.  Any meaningful traditions or things you are grateful for?

# MY LEGACY LETTER

# MY LEGACY LETTER

# My Legacy Letter

# NOTES:

# IMPORTANCE OF PERSISTENCE
# IN YOUR GROWTH

Persistence is defined as "firm or obstinate continuance in a course of action in spite of difficulty or opposition." A few synonyms for persistence include perseverance, tenacity, relentless, constantly, determination, and grit.

What comes to your mind when you hear the word persistence? Look back through your life. Can you share a time when you were persistent at achieving something? I bet you can.

Persistence can go all the way back to your birth. You were persistent in arriving in this world. You may not remember, but it took nine months of persistent growth and development to create you: Perfect, Wonderful, YOU!

*"One thing we all know, if one does not possess persistence, one does not achieve noteworthy success in any calling."*— NAPOLEON HILL

Persistence might be the time you learned something new, like learning to tie your shoelace, riding a bike, or swimming. Did you wake up one morning and those things just happened? Were those accomplishments all just handed to you? Probably not. You most likely needed to practice and repeat the same steps persistently over a period time, until you believed and desired to achieve it.

The point is that great things come to those who instill the habit of persistence. A good example of such a person is Rudy Ruettiger, the subject of the biographical film titled "Rudy" from 1993. Rudy dreamed of becoming a Notre Dame football player, but many people—including his own family—told him he was too small to play college football and did not have good enough grades to be accepted into Notre Dame.

Although Rudy faced a lot of opposition, even his own, his persistence over time beat the odds and he eventually achieved his dream of becoming a Notre Dame football player. This persistence is how many greats have achieved their success.

A quote that rings true is from Napoleon Hill in the book *Think and Grow Rich*. He states, "One thing we all know, if one does not possess persistence, one does not achieve noteworthy success in any calling."

Persistence is a part of being intentional about not giving up on the things you want to achieve. Do you have the characteristic of being persistent when you want something? If not, this is something you can grow and build upon. Ask yourself the following questions on the next page, so that they may help you grow and become more aware of your level of persistence.

# QUESTIONS TO HELP YOU UNDERSTAND
## YOUR LEVEL OF PERSISTENCE

1. Is persistence a *habit* for you? Why or why not? How can you cultivate it to become a habit and maintain it as a habit?

2. Do you have *belief* in your abilities? Do you trust that you can create and achieve the vision, goals, and dreams you desire?

3. Do you have the *willpower* to overcome opposition? What will keep you focused and concentrated during times of adversity and challenges?

4. When you want to achieve something, do you have a *decided heart*? Or do you worry and fear about your decision? How can or do you create a decided heart and let go of fear and worry?

5. Do you have a *"no quit"* or determined mentality when you want something? Or do you have a mentality of giving in or giving up when you hit a road block?

6. Do you believe in luck? Or do you believe that you put out an *intentional cause* to your actions and reap the effects? Do you believe preparation meets opportunity when you achieve what you want?

7. Are you willing to make sacrifices to stay persistent? What sacrifices are you willing to make to achieve your vision? (It could be time, money, networking, education, reading, etc., but not sacrifices to hurt you or others.)

# NOTES:

# CLOSING WORDS FOR ENCOURAGEMENT

**I want you to remember that you are <u>uniquely</u> and <u>wonderfully</u> made!**

This Growth Planner is a tool to help you **continuously** find focus and clarity for what is important in your life through your many seasons. Commit to it with a decided heart, and you will grow and achieve what you dream and desire.

It is not to be completed and put on a shelf to collect dust. If you truly want to live a life of fullness and greatness, you must be intentional about it. That means **consistently** envisioning and moving your plans of action towards growth every day, week, month, and year. A strong **faith,** along with **trust** and **belief** in yourself, is also vital.

Remember, this is not a competition. **Do not compare** yourself to others. A tree does not compare itself to a rose bush. Your life's journey is your own race.

**Don't idolize** the outcome or result; instead find daily peace that you are planting seeds and growing towards your goal. Perfect **peace** comes from knowing that you are making decisions from the heart.

Be **patient**, as nothing great has ever happened overnight. This world will fool you into believing that you can deliver immediate results. Even God did not create the universe in one day. He created new elements on different days and still is creating. There is no magic wand.

Focus on your daily factors that will keep your goal alive. They are a **positive attitude**, your **daily agenda**/action plan, and a **healthy environment** that will help your grow.

Be **disciplined** in how you start your day. Create new and **positive habits**. Be intentional about what you do each day and who you spend your time with.

Remain **grateful** in all things. Find gratitude in the storms, as storms will always exist in life. Don't let them stop you. Storms always end; they never last forever. Take those moments to **be teachable** moments. We can always gain a "silver lining" or exponential growth from our adversities.

**Share** your journey, goals, and dreams with others who will support you. One is too small a number for greatness. We were not put on this earth alone for a reason. Sharing with others who will support you can help you co-create your dreams and desires. They can also hold you accountable, which helps you push forward. You never know who may help you to that next level or through that road block.

**Finally, above all, rejoice in the journey of living. It is a gift to be alive!**

# APPENDIX

# APPENDIX A:
# GROWTH QUOTES – INTENTIONAL LIVING

"To reach your potential you must grow. And to grow, you must be highly intentional about it."

**John C. Maxwell**

"The best way to predict the future is to create it."

**Abraham Lincoln**

"Your vision becomes clear when you look inside your heart. Who looks outside, dreams. Who looks inside, awakens."

**Carl Jung**

"Change is inevitable. Growth is Intentional."

**John C. Maxwell**

"Perseverance. It's hard to beat a person who never gives up."

**Babe Ruth**

"In order to carry a positive action, we must develop here a positive vision."

**Dalai Lama**

"Surround yourself by people who are only going to lift you higher."

**Oprah Winfrey**

"You will never change your life until you change something you do daily."

**John C. Maxwell**

# APPENDIX B:
# GROWTH AFFIRMATIONS – INTENTIONAL LIVING

I am at peace with the day. I flow with life easily and effortlessly.

I wake up with gratitude for each day. I live each day intentionally and with purpose.

I am living my best life now. I am enjoying the journey.

I am wonderfully and perfectly made. I love myself.

Everything I do is a success. I prosper no matter where I am or what I am doing.

I am transforming into the best ME. I trust life.

My decisions are always perfect for me. Only good comes into my life.

I am powerful, capable and open to the wisdom, love and light that shines within me.

I move peacefully and happily towards my growth each day. Each day brings wonderful new surprises.

I am creating only good habits that are transforming me into my greatness.

I have greatness in me. I am more powerful than I know. I am joyful and love life.

I trust the process of life. Life supports me and brings me only good and positive experiences.

I go beyond my fears and limitations. I am open to the new and changing.

# APPENDIX C: 12 MONTHLY REFLECTION WORKSHEETS – INTENTIONAL LIVING

## Monthly Check in on Growth

1. How do you feel about your growth and intentionality this past month?

2. What can you improve on this next month?

3. Were there any lessons learned this last month?

4. Is there anything you need to add or change for next month?

5. Did you daily maintain a positive attitude, reflect on your vision, express gratitude?

**Month 1 Growth Tree**
*My Monthly Achievement Board*

**Environment I Created**

**Monthly Check in on Growth**

1. How do you feel about your growth and intentionality this past month?

2. What can you improve on this next month?

3. Were there any lessons learned this last month?

4. Is there anything you need to add or change for next month?

5. Did you daily maintain a positive attitude, reflect on your vision, express gratitude?

**Month 2 Growth Tree**
*My Monthly Achievement Board*

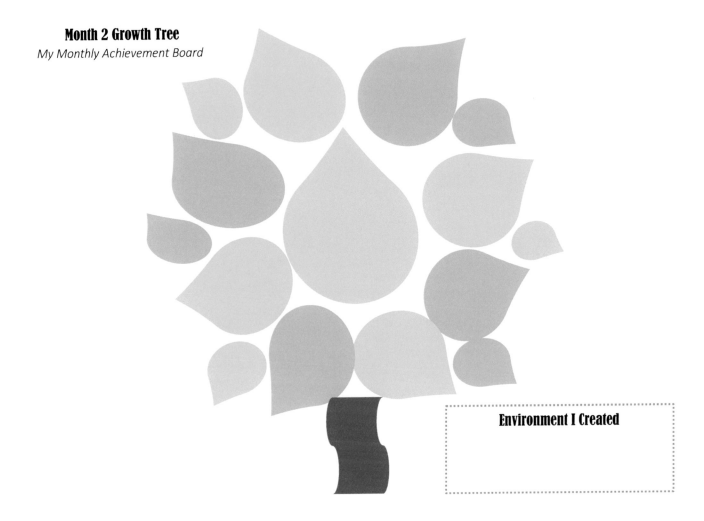

**Environment I Created**

## Monthly Check in on Growth

1. How do you feel about your growth and intentionality this past month?

2. What can you improve on this next month?

3. Were there any lessons learned this last month?

4. Is there anything you need to add or change for next month?

5. Did you daily maintain a positive attitude, reflect on your vision, express gratitude?

### Month 3 Growth Tree
*My Monthly Achievement Board*

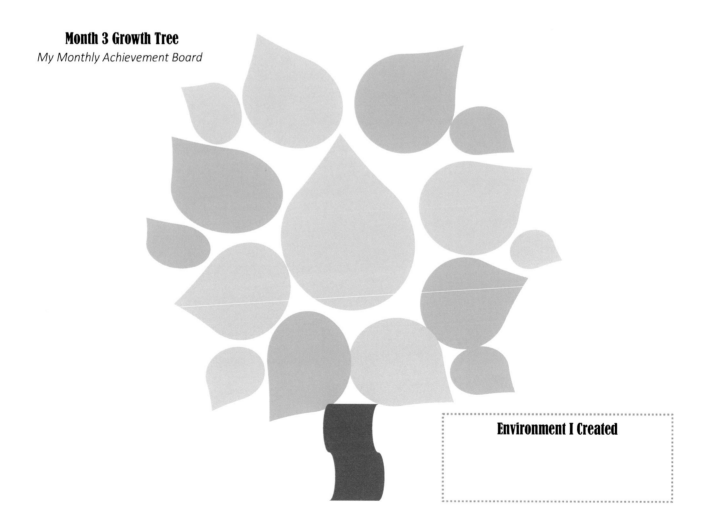

**Environment I Created**

## Monthly Check in on Growth

1. How do you feel about your growth and intentionality this past month?

2. What can you improve on this next month?

3. Were there any lessons learned this last month?

4. Is there anything you need to add or change for next month?

5. Did you daily maintain a positive attitude, reflect on your vision, express gratitude?

### Month 4 Growth Tree
*My Monthly Achievement Board*

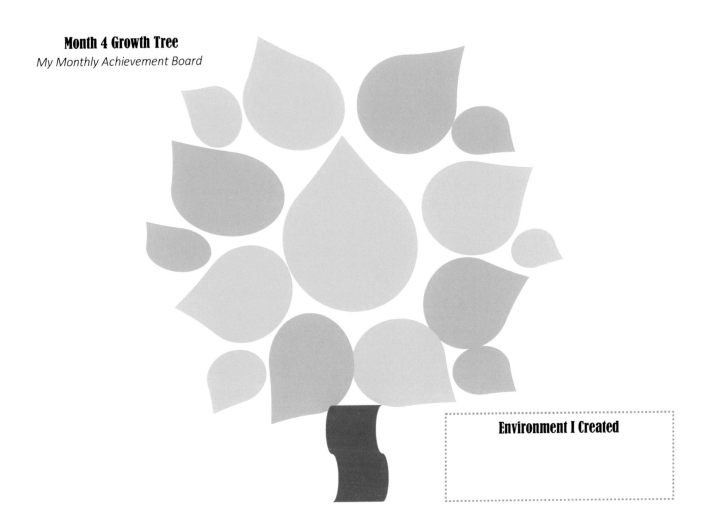

**Environment I Created**

# MONTH 5 REFLECTION WORKSHEET – INTENTIONAL LIVING

## Monthly Check in on Growth

1. How do you feel about your growth and intentionality this past month?

2. What can you improve on this next month?

3. Were there any lessons learned this last month?

4. Is there anything you need to add or change for next month?

5. Did you daily maintain a positive attitude, reflect on your vision, express gratitude?

**Month 5 Growth Tree**
*My Monthly Achievement Board*

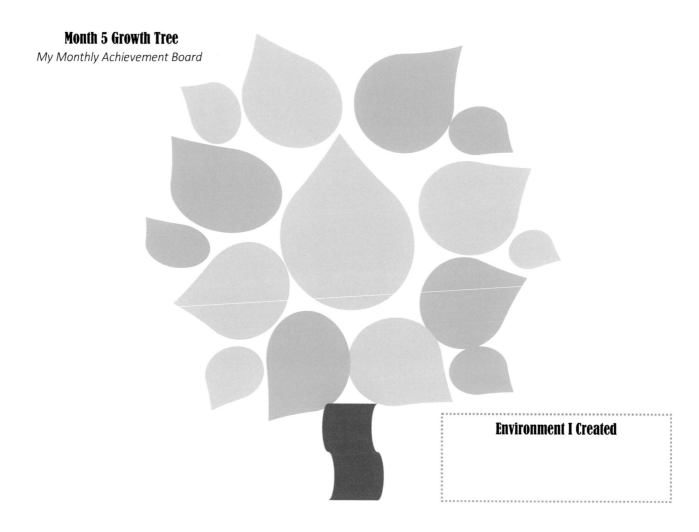

**Environment I Created**

**Monthly Check in on Growth**

1.  How do you feel about your growth and intentionality this past month?

2.  What can you improve on this next month?

3.  Were there any lessons learned this last month?

4.  Is there anything you need to add or change for next month?

5.  Did you daily maintain a positive attitude, reflect on your vision, express gratitude?

**Month 6 Growth Tree**
*My Monthly Achievement Board*

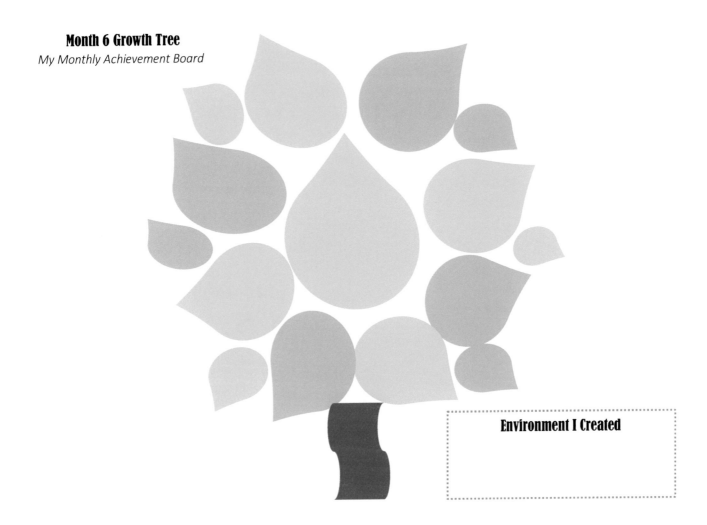

**Environment I Created**

### Monthly Check in on Growth

1. How do you feel about your growth and intentionality this past month?

2. What can you improve on this next month?

3. Were there any lessons learned this last month?

4. Is there anything you need to add or change for next month?

5. Did you daily maintain a positive attitude, reflect on your vision, express gratitude?

**Month 7 Growth Tree**
*My Monthly Achievement Board*

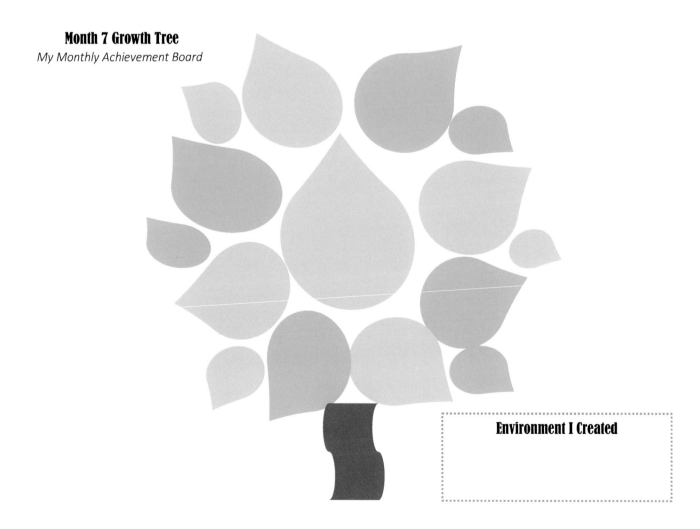

**Environment I Created**

**Monthly Check in on Growth**

1. How do you feel about your growth and intentionality this past month?

2. What can you improve on this next month?

3. Were there any lessons learned this last month?

4. Is there anything you need to add or change for next month?

5. Did you daily maintain a positive attitude, reflect on your vision, express gratitude?

**Month 8 Growth Tree**
*My Monthly Achievement Board*

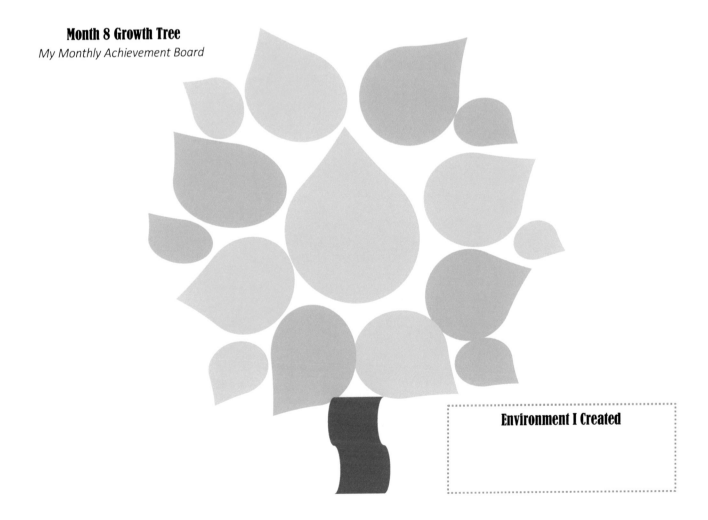

**Environment I Created**

## Monthly Check in on Growth

1. How do you feel about your growth and intentionality this past month?

2. What can you improve on this next month?

3. Were there any lessons learned this last month?

4. Is there anything you need to add or change for next month?

5. Did you daily maintain a positive attitude, reflect on your vision, express gratitude?

### Month 9 Growth Tree
*My Monthly Achievement Board*

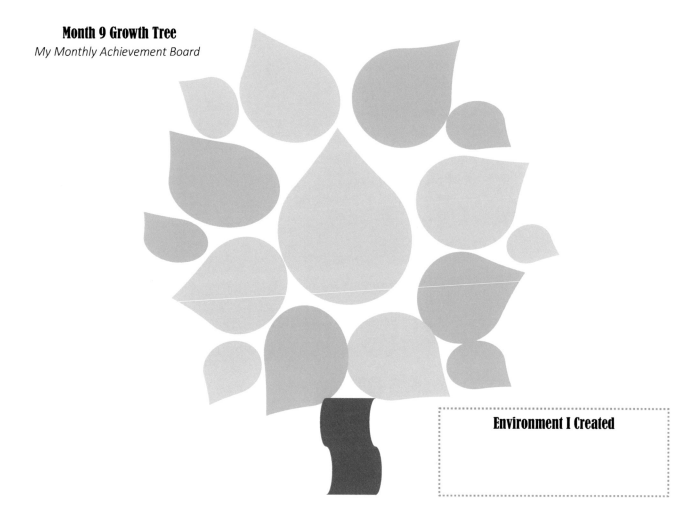

**Environment I Created**

**Monthly Check in on Growth**

1. How do you feel about your growth and intentionality this past month?

2. What can you improve on this next month?

3. Were there any lessons learned this last month?

4. Is there anything you need to add or change for next month?

5. Did you daily maintain a positive attitude, reflect on your vision, express gratitude?

**Month 10 Growth Tree**
*My Monthly Achievement Board*

**Environment I Created**

## Monthly Check in on Growth

1. How do you feel about your growth and intentionality this past month?

2. What can you improve on this next month?

3. Were there any lessons learned this last month?

4. Is there anything you need to add or change for next month?

5. Did you daily maintain a positive attitude, reflect on your vision, express gratitude?

### Month 11 Growth Tree
*My Monthly Achievement Board*

**Environment I Created**

### Monthly Check in on Growth

1. How do you feel about your growth and intentionality this past month?

2. What can you improve on this next month?

3. Were there any lessons learned this last month?

4. Is there anything you need to add or change for next month?

5. Did you daily maintain a positive attitude, reflect on your vision, express gratitude?

### Month 12 Growth Tree
*My Monthly Achievement Board*

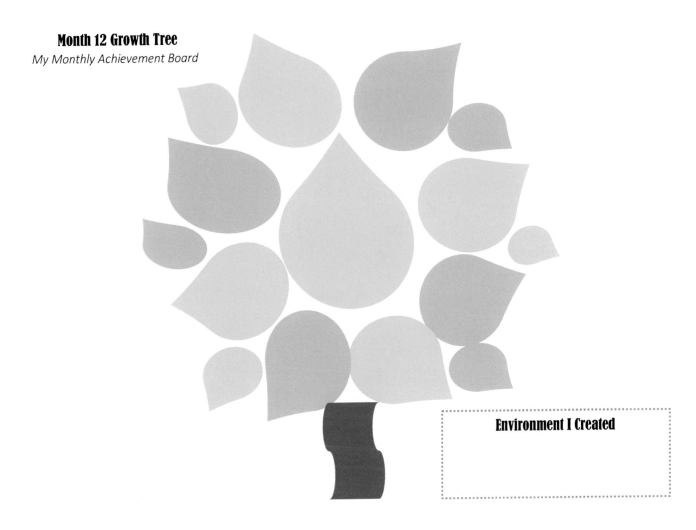

### Environment I Created

# Appendix D: Long Term Growth Tree Vision Board

If you could be anything, do anything, have anything, what would it be? This is your Growth Tree – Your Vision Board. You can write your visions into each leaf or add pictures.

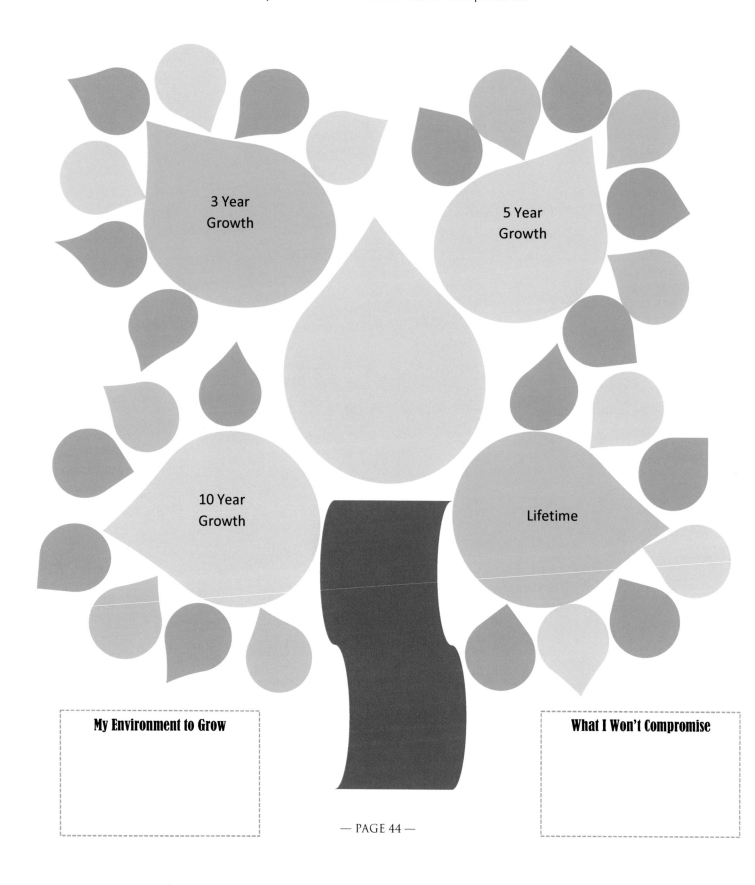

3 Year Growth

5 Year Growth

10 Year Growth

Lifetime

My Environment to Grow

What I Won't Compromise

# Appendix E: End of Year Reflection Worksheet – Intentional Living

## Things I am *Thankful for...*

## My BIG Contributions...

## Favorite **Memories...**

## My Achievements...

## Hard Lesson I Learned...

## Things I want to get better at...

## What I am Most Proud of...

# Recommended Reading: Resources to Grow – Intentional Living

*(in no special order)*

*Intentional Living: Choosing a Life That Matters*
by **John C. Maxwell**

*Start with Why: How Great Leaders Inspire Everyone to Take Action*
by **Simon Sinek**

*Grit*
by **Angela Duckworth**

*Man's Search for Meaning*
by **Viktor E. Frankl**

*Think and Grow Rich*
by **Napoleon Hill**

*The Power is Within You*
by **Louise Hay**

*Today Matters*
by **John C. Maxwell**

*The Power of Intention*
by **Wayne Dyer**

*Relentless: From Good to Great to Unstoppable*
by **Tim S. Grover**

*Succeed: How We Can Reach Our Goals*
by **Heidi Grant Holvorson**

*The Brain That Changes Itself: Stories of Personal Triumph from the Frontiers of Brain Science*
by **Norman Doidge**

*Wishes Fulfilled*
by **Wayne Dyer**

# ABOUT THE AUTHOR:
## AMY WATTS – YOUR ENCOURAGEMENT COACH

**Amy Watts** is an International Business and Personal Coach, empowering personal and professional achievement through interpersonal, practical, highly effective, and proven methods.

Her passion lies in helping individuals, businesses, and teams find their strengths and develop their opportunities to grow in their greatness. This is achieved through a model she uses to assess their current position, understand their strengths, and customize a "Vision Plan Grow" roadmap to achieve it.

Amy held executive leadership positions with start-ups and top 100 Fortune companies before becoming an entrepreneur with continued growth and success. Using the knowledge, skills, and tools she learned over 20 years, she started her own coaching business.

She is now living out her passion. Today, Amy is transforming clients on six of seven continents to reach incredible levels of performance, growth, awareness, accountability, and transformation.

Amy helps her clients recognize their opportunities and push past fears to overcome blocks from limited, modeled thinking. She believes everyone should be encouraged and empowered to know and achieve their greatness.

To learn more about Amy and how she can help you, visit her online:

VisionPlanGrow.com
facebook.com/visionplangrow

Made in the USA
Middletown, DE
14 June 2018